Sleeping with a Monster: My Story of Survival

by Aneta Sproles

While every precaution has been taken in the preparation of this book, the publisher assumes no responsibility for errors or omissions, or for damages resulting from the use of the information contained herein.

SLEEPING WITH A MONSTER: MY STORY OF SURVIVAL

First edition. October 25, 2024.

ISBN: 979-8227836113

Written by Aneta Sproles.

Table of Contents

Introduction 1

Preface 3

Chapter 1: The Beginning of Aneta & Darnell 5

Chapter 2: The Marriage and Turning Point 9

Chapter 3: The Masks Begin to Peel 13

Chapter 4: Terror Escalates 17

Chapter 5: Darnell the Devil 25

Chapter 6: Hell Visits Me on Earth 29

Chapter 7: My Monster Has No Remorse 35

Chapter 8: Being Hunted & Divorcing My Monster 39

Chapter 9: Breaking Free from the Monster 43

This book is dedicated to my six beautiful children, who were my beacon of hope as I endured years of abuse. I fervently prayed for survival, not wanting my children to attend my funeral due to the actions of the man they knew as Mr. Darnell. I made it through. My love for you has been the driving force that kept me strong and alive. Mom loves you. To my amazing six.

Introduction

The journey to freedom begins with a single, terrifying step. In "Sleeping with a Monster: My Story of Survival", I, Aneta Sproles, take you through the darkest chapters of my life, where fear, pain, and confusion were my constant companions. This book is not just about recounting the horror I lived through; it is about the strength and resilience that carried me through the storm.

I wrote this book to give a voice to those who have been silenced by abuse. To the women and men who feel trapped in a nightmare they can't seem to wake up from, I want you to know that you are not alone. My story is your story. My pain is your pain. And my survival can be your survival too.

As you read through these pages, you will see not only the depths of despair but also the glimmers of hope that guided me toward the light. This book is a testament to the power of the human spirit and the belief that no matter how dark the night, the dawn will come. I invite you to join me on this journey—one of pain, healing, and, ultimately, triumph.

Preface

In the depths of darkness, where despair threatened to suffocate me, I found the faintest glimmer of hope—a hope that eventually blossomed into the strength to reclaim my life. *Sleeping with a Monster: My Story of Survival* is not just a recounting of my experiences with abuse; it is a testament to the resilience of the human spirit and the power of healing.

As I reflect on my journey, I realize that sharing my story is as much for me as it is for you. It's a cathartic release, a way to confront the shadows of my past while illuminating a path toward understanding and healing. I wrote this book with the hope that it will resonate with those who have felt trapped in their own lives, silenced by the weight of trauma. My story is a reminder that there is life after abuse—a vibrant life filled with possibilities and joy.

Throughout these pages, you will witness my struggles and triumphs. You will see the effects of living in fear, the emotional scars left by my abuser, and the journey toward reclaiming my identity. My story is not one of shame but of courage; it is a celebration of survival, resilience, and the pursuit of happiness.

I want to extend my hand to anyone who feels lost, alone, or afraid. You are not alone in your pain. I invite you to walk with me through the chapters of my life, to feel the emotions I once buried, and to find the strength within yourself to break free from your own chains. Together, we can navigate the complexities of healing, discovering that our past does not dictate our future.

As you read my story, I hope you find validation in your own experiences and the courage to speak your truth. It is time to shed the weight of silence and embrace the healing power of our stories. In sharing my truth, I aspire to ignite a spark of hope and inspire others to take the brave steps toward their own liberation.

Let this book be a beacon of light, guiding you through your darkest moments and reminding you that survival is possible. We can rise from the ashes, reclaim our power, and create lives filled with love, joy, and purpose.

Chapter 1: The Beginning of Aneta & Darnell

One day at work, I strolled around, reflecting on the happy couples I saw. I couldn't believe I was divorced again, a mother of six, feeling like I had given my all to my last marriage. After a lot of thought, I decided to work at a day center for individuals with special needs, where my education and experience could make a difference. Two weeks after applying, I received a call offering me the job.

I had been there about four months when I noticed a new guy during my break. He was tall and strong, walking with another employee. "Who's that?" I wondered, realizing he was being interviewed. As I drove past in my beat-up truck, we locked eyes, and I felt a wave of embarrassment about my vehicle's condition. "There's no way he'd be interested in me," I thought.

I didn't think much of it after that, assuming I'd see him around if he got hired. A couple of weeks later, I started getting his transportation slips mixed up with mine. Unbeknownst to me, he worked right next door. I would take the slips to him, joking about the mix-ups, and he'd respond with a smile.

One day, as we were on our transportation routes, I had a bold thought: "What if I asked him out?" Chili's was my favorite restaurant, especially for their two-for-$20 special, so when I saw him drive by, I stopped him and said, "Hey, how about two-for-$20?" He smiled and replied, "OK, wait until I get back." Since my route was longer, I was surprised to find his car waiting for me when I returned. He wanted my number! I couldn't believe it—the two-for-$20 worked!

That's how it all began. We exchanged numbers and started texting, getting to know each other. I felt a mix of excitement and nerves; I had only been single for a few months after a significant break-up. But with Darnell, everything felt different. We talked often, and though his name was common—reminding me of people from my past—I chose not to judge him based on that.

In the beginning, Darnell and I became like best friends. We frequently went on dates, exchanged gifts for ourselves and our kids, and held family events at my house. I even took Darnell's oldest daughter to parties, hoping to bond with his children. It felt like nothing could break us apart. Our relationship was fast-paced and filled with joy, with Darnell always surprising me with little things I liked.

I reciprocated by giving him custom gifts based on what he enjoyed. It felt like I had found the love of my life. I didn't mind how quickly we moved in together; it felt right. We even navigated COVID together, spending quality time and having fun. But as swiftly as our happiness blossomed, it soon turned to horror. Just six weeks into our relationship, Darnell hit me for the first time.

The happiness we had shared faded, and the physical and verbal abuse began. I couldn't believe the man who had pursued me so eagerly was now hurting me. I tried to make him happy, planning special things, but the abuse overshadowed everything.

I remember introducing Darnell to my mother for the first time. As soon as she saw him, she yelled, "Not him, no!" My mother had never met Darnell, but her instinct was strong. She saw something in him that I couldn't. I brushed it off, saying, "Mom, it's OK. You just don't want me with anyone." But she insisted, "No, something's wrong. Watch out for him. He's an opportunist."

Looking back, I realize I should have listened to her. If I had, I might have avoided the abuse that followed.

Chapter 2: The Marriage and Turning Point

After Darnell and I exchanged numbers that night, I was completely mesmerized. I couldn't stop talking about him to everyone I knew—this incredible guy with kids who seemed perfect. I remember thinking, "Darnell is it." It felt like everything was falling into place.

A few days later, I finally went over to his house for pizza. Meeting his kids was a big deal for me; I always took that seriously. I had my own daughter, Kia, and I missed her so much. I remember thinking how fast everything was moving, but I was excited.

As the evening went on, I decided to spend the night. I didn't want to come off as someone who does one-night stands, so I started on the couch, but eventually, I ended up in his bedroom. One thing led to another, and we found ourselves in bed together. From that moment, everything felt like a whirlwind. We went on dates, spent time at each other's homes, and his spontaneous pop-up visits made me feel special. I thought it was his way of expressing love, showering me with gifts and attention.

Months passed, and we decided to take a trip to Vegas. We dropped the kids off and drove there, laughing so hard that I almost peed my pants. I felt like we were best friends, even though we had only been together for a short time. After checking into our hotel, we found ourselves in a chapel, following a guy on a scooter to get married. It was surreal—one moment we were joking, and the next, we were exchanging vows. We were officially married, but it didn't feel as impactful since we had already been living together.

In the beginning, Darnell showed me a side of himself that was loving and caring. But there were also moments of physical and verbal abuse that I tried to overlook, telling myself he was just stressed. I kept these incidents to myself, convincing myself that everything would be fine.

Once we got married, the situation took a turn for the worse. I became pregnant, but the trauma of the relationship and the abuse led to a miscarriage. I struggled to tell Darnell about it, fearing it would hurt him. He believed I was still pregnant, and I felt trapped in my silence. I had already experienced the trauma of losing custody of my own children, and I was still processing that pain.

As our relationship continued, I discovered that Darnell was not the supportive partner I thought he was. He promised to help me fight to get my children back, but behind my back, he was telling the courts I was unfit to be a mother. I was devastated when I learned that he was actively working against me.

I had married Darnell believing we could build a happy family together. I threw myself into being a good stepmother, hoping to create a loving environment. But as I tried to maintain a semblance of normalcy, Darnell's anger grew. I began to notice the red flags—his kindness seemed more like a façade.

Over time, the anger escalated. He would blame me for his behavior, and I felt increasingly isolated. I found myself in terrifying situations, like when he violently slammed my head against a door, and his daughters witnessed the abuse. That was a turning point for me; I realized the severity of what I was enduring.

Darnell's manipulation was calculated, and it took me a long time to recognize it. The trauma I faced was overwhelming, and I felt like I was living in a nightmare, confronting my own personal monster. Reflecting on my experiences, I began to understand that I was just one of many victims caught in Darnell's web of deceit and manipulation.

As I recount these moments, I'm grateful to be alive. I survived a situation that many don't, and while I still carry the scars, I'm determined to reclaim my life and share my story.

Chapter 3: The Masks Begin to Peel

They say the company you keep matters, and Darnell's friends were a reflection of his troubled life. One of his closest friends, Lenny, was a drug dealer. I often wondered, "Darnell, why do you associate with people like this?" But he would shrug it off, saying, "These are my friends; I've known them forever."

One night, we went over to Lenny's house, where he offered Darnell ecstasy pills. Until that moment, I had never tried any drugs in my life. When Darnell asked if I wanted to try some, I hesitated, but feeling pressure to support him as his wife, I eventually said yes. I remember thinking, "God, please don't let me regret this." Darnell broke off a piece of the pill and handed it to me. As I swallowed it, I felt a wave of panic wash over me; I was stepping into a world I knew nothing about.

Darnell had a history with drugs long before I came into his life, and for him, this was just part of the cycle. For me, it was terrifying. As we both found ourselves cooped up in the house, overwhelmed by the stresses of our children and our crumbling marriage, the drugs became a temporary escape.

One day, Darnell suggested I try something new. "What else could we possibly try?" I asked, already reeling from ecstasy. He pulled out a pipe and said I needed to smoke it. I was taken aback. I had never smoked anything before. Yet here I was, trying to be the supportive wife, trying to bond with him.

It wasn't until later, during a particularly dark time, that I learned just how deeply Darnell had been involved with drugs. When he introduced me to methamphetamines, I was horrified. I felt trapped in a marriage that had turned from a joyful partnership to a chaotic nightmare. Darnell was not just using drugs; he was also physically abusive. My family had essentially disowned me, so it felt like Darnell was all I had.

What started as a misguided attempt to connect with my husband quickly turned into a coping mechanism for the abuse I was enduring. I remember one particular incident when Darnell offered me cocaine in front of his friends. As I consumed it, I could see the smug expressions on their faces. They laughed as I spiraled into an angry, jittery state, their amusement making the situation feel even more degrading.

The abuse escalated dramatically. I remember an argument when Darnell rammed my head into the bathroom door. His daughters rushed in, screaming for him to let me go, but he held me there for what felt like an eternity. Blood trickled down my forehead, and in that moment, I realized just how serious the situation had become.

Darnell would often provoke me in front of his children, painting me as the villain in their eyes, even though I had always cared for them. He manipulated his kids to see me as the enemy, while I had genuinely loved them and wanted to be a good stepmother. His efforts to turn them against me were both baffling and heartbreaking.

The most insidious part of his manipulation was how he would speak about my children, who have special needs, in the most derogatory terms. During fights, he'd hurl horrible names at them, and I couldn't fathom how someone who claimed to love me could so callously attack the children I had given birth to. I will never forget the moment he accused my son of attempting to harm his daughter—an outrageous lie stemming from a simple, innocent interaction. It infuriated me to see how Darnell could weaponize my children's disabilities to hurt me.

Then there was the time I had to attend my father's funeral out of state. Darnell acted as if he couldn't fly, refusing to support me during such a difficult time. My family had warned me about his abusive nature, but I didn't listen. Even when I arrived at my father's funeral, Darnell continued to call, stirring up chaos and trying to bring me back home. The day before the funeral, I had a huge argument with my family due to his manipulation and left them feeling hurt and frustrated.

When I finally watched my father's service online, Darnell laughed and played video games, seemingly indifferent to my pain. Hours after the funeral, when I was still grieving, he demanded sex, showing no empathy for my loss. His behavior was that of a monster, devoid of heart or compassion.

I will never forget the smirks and the cruelty Darnell displayed, especially in my darkest moments. The masks he wore began to peel away, revealing the true nature of the man I had married.

Chapter 4: Terror Escalates

Darnell started early on tracking my phones and being able to see my messages with people, and I noticed he started to track my phones more and be able to look on his phone and see my phone messages. I was sending to people when I would be texting my friend and I'd be texting my colleagues and coworkers about the abuse that Darnell was subjecting me to. I noticed I could always tell that somehow I had my phone tracker linked to his because when I would text somebody about the abuse, Darnell would somehow know what I was texting to people and he would always come and say something to me after I was sending messages out, and I would never forget that every time I talked to somebody, text Darnell would say something to me and ask me who was I texting and what we were talking about.

Darnell had a very bad obsession with always wanting to see my phone, always wanting to know what I was doing. He would track my phone to know where I was. I never had a moment when he didn't know where I was. I never gave Darnell consent to track me, but that's what an abuser does. He would always keep track of my messages. He'd know when I was texting my coworkers and friends about the abuse because he would manipulate my phone. Whenever he got frustrated because I wouldn't let him see my phone, or he didn't have a tracking device at the time, or there wasn't an app connected to my phone, he'd often break my phones. He would put my phones into certain modes where I wouldn't be able to call out or text, leaving me isolated with Darnell, unable to contact anyone. It was really disturbing.

I noticed that when I asked Darnell for his phone, he would hit me or push me, calling me horrifying names. It would turn into the biggest fight, but he always wanted to keep track of me and know what I was doing. It was a sick, vicious cycle.

I could only imagine all the affairs and terrible things Darnell was doing, discovering by accident the horrific things he hid in his phone. For someone to try to take away your freedom and your sense of peace will be one of the biggest regrets of my entire life.

I remember the times I finally managed to get away from Darnell, even if only temporarily. Each time I escaped, he would come after me. I recall one instance when I was so stressed that I wanted to leave for good. In a moment of desperation, I lied to Darnell and told him I was pregnant by another man. While I knew I wasn't actually pregnant, I hoped this would drive him away. However, he continued to pursue me. I would enter programs for domestic violence, or they would place me in hotels, but Darnell would always find me, causing disruptions that led to my being kicked out of those programs and forced to return to him. It felt like a terrifying cycle from which I could never escape, leaving me to wander the streets.

Eventually, I sought help at a shelter because Darnell had once again manipulated the situation. He obtained a false order of protection for a house that was solely in my name. The police and the courts prohibited me from returning to my home while Darnell remained there, leaving them to determine who was telling the truth. I ended up on the streets for weeks, sleeping outdoors, begging for food, and moving from shelter to shelter. I endured harrowing weeks fighting to regain my house. By the time they finally informed Darnell that he had to leave, he had barricaded himself inside. He refused to exit, even with the police and the landlord outside.

I remember receiving the call informing me that Darnell would not leave. They said we would have to find another way to deal with the situation. The police eventually left, and I followed them, overwhelmed with stress and frustration. I couldn't understand how he could remain in my house while I was left powerless. The police allowed him to stay there.

When they finally managed to get Darnell out and I was able to enter the house days later, I was struck by the terrible smell and the state of disarray. I couldn't believe how much Darnell had trashed the place. Essentially, everything I owned was gone, and the house was in ruins. The following day, the landlord placed something on my door. When I stepped outside to check my mail, I discovered an eviction notice stating that there had been 400 police reports over the years Darnell and I had lived there, even after he moved out and removed his name from the lease. The police had been called to the house numerous times due to Darnell's physical abuse, yet they did nothing. The only time they took action was when Darnell went to court and lied about me, submitting false documents.

At that moment, I felt utterly helpless. Why was I being evicted when I was the victim? Why was the man who everyone recognized as my abuser—the manipulator, the terrifying monster in my life—getting away with everything? Those thoughts consumed me.

One day when I was driving with Darnell, we got into an argument as we were driving he pulled over he locked the doors, and as he thought I was about to try to get out as I reach for the handle, he was punching me in the chest, and then he took a hot torch, and he began hitting me in the arm, burning my arm. I remember, he just kept cursing me out as he was punching me, repeating the chest and the arm. He continues to constantly burn me with the torch on my arm, hitting me repeatedly. Every time I try to reach for the door to get out of the car, even though I was right down the street from my apartment I was willing to walk, but he did not want me to get out of the car, and I began to sit in the car and cry the more he will punch me in the chest and hit me with the hot torch, it was more he was hitting me and he was getting me crying wanting to get away from it wanting to get out the car escaped abuse that Darnell was doing to me.

I remember one day I was sitting in a store with Darnell in the parking lot talking and we were around the corner from some house. He claimed that he lived at the time, and I remember he began to just be so evil to me out of the blue when I was talking to him, everything I said was irritating Darnell and I will never forget. I got so frustrated, and I told Darnell I was ready to take him home and I will be driving back to his house to drop Darnell off as I got ready to turn the corner in my car. Darnell told me to stop the car in the middle of the street and he said look. Somethings going on and I remember just turning and looking thinking that something was going on and by the time I turned back around Darnell had a shirt Wrapped around my neck and he was choking me, and I could barely breathe and then he snatched my glasses off my face and threw them on the ground to the point where they broke inside the car and I remember watching as I kept screaming and the neighbors and the people on the block who saw me and what was happening didn't even call for help and I remember Darnell got out of my car and I just sped away crying. I could barely see one of my lenses was broken and I picked my glasses up on the floor And I drove to my apartment with my glasses. My throat was so sore from choking me with the T-shirt and it was another humiliating time of abuse that served at the hands of my Darnell.

One night at our hotel room, I would never forget Darnell kept punching me telling me to smoke more drugs and I didn't want to do it and I remembered that after I finally started to cry and I gave, and he told me to add fear he then got up he punch me and hitting me and every time I try to get up and get out the way he was standing in front of me to bombard me and barricade me in and they hit me again and I remember one of these particular hits because he punched me so hard that I fell between the bed and the dresser and I was in so much pain and I thought that the drugs were numb the pain, but I still feel pain through being high on Drugs it was another traumatic episode of abuse. I was suffering and I remember the whole night he just kept talking to me and yelling at me and hitting me and by the time I finally got back conscious and I woke up the next day all of a sudden he turned into this guy who he forgot he had done the night before how he had maliciously attacked me how he had beat on me again how he had hit me and forced me to do drugs , and so many prayers. Every day Darnell would be abusive. I prayed to God to let me live and eventually get out.

I remember when me and Darnell were homeless and I remember we went to rent a hotel room together, and I will never forget. Darnell was so upset with me, and I was sitting on the toilet. He walked in the bathroom and begin repeatedly, punching me in the head to the point where I feel like I could die I remember stumbling out of the bathroom as he kept yelling at me as I was walking into the bed, and I fell in the bed and I'll be foaming at the mouth and Darnell just said to lay there and not say a word and I better not tell anybody and I remember feeling like I was dying and I remember having flashbacks of me and my children in my head as I laid on the pillow foaming and so much pain in my head because he had so many blows with his fist to my head, believe a man could be so vile and vicious like that and I thought I was going to lose my life that day in the hotel and I just remember how you kept saying you better not tell anybody you better not say what happened. You better not call anybody, don't start texting on your phone because when I was texting my phone, Darnell would get scared feeling like I was texting people to alert the authorities that he had done something else to me.

I remember one day we were arguing in the house, and Darnell always was known to carry guns and I remember we were arguing and I was on the other side of the bed and Darnell grabbed his gun and pointed at me and I was so afraid because he was so angry and raised with a gun in his hand that I urinated on myself, and I began to scream and I remember I only had a T-shirt and I had no pants on And I remember running downstairs just to put myself in the doorway in case he shot me and the neighbors would know what was going on or maybe me being a friend the door was stopping shooting at me just couldn't pull a gun, but what I would learn is that this would not be the last time that Darnell pulled a gun on me and put my life in danger. I remember constantly contacting the police about all the abuse I went through with Darnell, and I remember how they were just called Darnell. Ask him if he did it and Darnell would lie and say he didn't abuse me and I remember feeling so frustrated for years as I watched the police me to be tortured and abused by Darnell and how he would laugh and brag and say how he was just untouchable, and he just could get away with anything and I think about all the nights that I suffered ,crying and hallucinating because of the drugs. Suffering from the drugs he forcefully put into my body, going through pain from the abuse of him hitting me going to the pain of him, choking me just remembering how he would hit me like I was a man, and he will punch me and all the time where I would feel like I was going to die. To See Darnell just happy and OK and having no remorse it's like abusing me. Darnell turns into a monster, something inhumane, something dark. I thought if I loved him a little more, he'd stop abusing me, but I had to realize that no matter how much I love Darnell and how much I tried to love him Darnell was still an abuser. That's who he was. That's what he did and no amount of love, and I wish I would've realized would've stopped the fact that I was sleeping with the monster who could not help showing his face and showing his evil ways. Every chance he got because he felt like I was helpless.

Chapter 5: Darnell the Devil

I remember the moment Darnell moved out and took his name off the lease, leaving the house in my name. What followed was a whirlwind of vengeance from him, despite being the one who chose to leave for Lenny's mother. Darnell began a campaign of harassment, damaging the house and making false police reports against me.

One incident stands out vividly. Darnell injured himself and accused me of abusing him, leading to my arrest. I had never been in trouble with the law before, and it was surreal to find myself in handcuffs, all while Darnell stood by, laughing with his friends. The police were disappointing, failing to see me as the victim in this twisted game.

Darnell didn't stop there. He secured a restraining order by lying to the court, claiming I still lived at the house, even though it was legally mine. He continued to orchestrate my arrests, reveling in the chaos he created. I remember the times he broke into my home, selling off my belongings—things I had worked hard for before I even met him. It was a betrayal that impacted my life in ways I couldn't begin to fathom.

Each false accusation Darnell made chipped away at my sanity. He would mock me, boast about how no one would uncover his lies. The police, instead of recognizing the real perpetrator, saw me as the villain, leaving me feeling utterly powerless.

One night, after a particularly harrowing experience in jail, I found myself in the hospital. Darnell called, pretending to be concerned. Unbeknownst to me, he still had a protection order against me. When he picked me up, his face held a sinister look. As soon as we arrived at the house, he threatened, "You're going to jail," and took off running. Panic surged through me as I fled down the street, desperate for safety, terrified that he had set me up once again.

Darnell's abusive behavior escalated as he became more brazen with his affairs. At first, he was secretive, but over time, as he tightened his grip on me, he became openly disrespectful. He would text other women right in front of me, calling out their physical attributes while belittling me. As a Black woman, hearing him express admiration for women of other races was not just painful—it was humiliating.

Despite everything, I had stood by Darnell during his lowest moments, providing support and love. Yet, he repaid my loyalty with constant betrayal. My family would often question my choices, urging me to leave him, but the reality was far more complicated. I was caught in a cycle of addiction, abuse, and isolation.

Darnell had unresolved trauma from his childhood, which he projected onto me. He harbored a disturbing disdain for Black women, including me—his wife. It was incomprehensible. He had children with a Black woman before me, yet he spewed derogatory comments about my race and made me feel inferior. It felt like a cruel joke.

Darnell was a master manipulator. One moment, he would shower me with affection, and the next, he would turn violent. It left me confused and emotionally drained. I often found myself asking, "Why are you doing this to me?" But his responses always deflected blame back onto me, distorting reality to maintain control.

As time passed, I began researching narcissistic personality disorder, suspecting that Darnell fit the profile. When I mentioned it, he would explode in rage, revealing just how deeply his issues ran. I confided in friends, who noted his disrespectful behavior, but I felt trapped, isolated from those who cared about me.

The psychological toll was immense. Darnell would harm himself, using it as a threat against me. "If you don't do what I say, I'll call the police and tell them you have a mental health condition," he would say, instilling fear that no one would believe me.

Living in a chaotic, filthy apartment filled with trash, I would find myself begging neighbors for food. Darnell reveled in my humiliation, taunting me as I struggled to maintain some semblance of normalcy.

Every day was a battle against his manipulation and the trauma he inflicted. I felt like I was living in a nightmare with no escape, questioning how I ended up in such a dark place. Darnell's ability to twist the narrative left me feeling helpless, and I began to realize that I needed to break free from this cycle of abuse before it consumed me entirely.

Chapter 6: Hell Visits Me on Earth

I remember when I decided to move to a suburb, Darnell would show up at my door every single day. He wasn't coming because he loved me or was sad that we were separated. Instead, he came to argue and fight, often reeking of another woman's scent, just to flaunt his freedom and do as he please. For four months straight, he showed up daily, sitting on my bed and insisting that I needed to do drugs, claiming that I wasn't okay or happy because I wasn't using them. I would tell him, "I don't want to do that, Darnell." But he would threaten me or say horrific things.

I'll never forget the night my mother told me she woke up in her sleep feeling that something was wrong, though she didn't know what it was. That night, Darnell had taken some blue pills laced with fentanyl and shoved them up my nose, trying to overdose me. He was vicious, like a monster, and he took pleasure in inflicting trauma, whether physically or with drugs. As he forced the blue pills into my nose, I felt like I was dying, drifting in and out of consciousness while he laughed and poured water on my face. Days later, when I told my mother what happened, she said, "I was up praying for you. I didn't know what was going on, but I knew something wasn't right, and I had a feeling Darnell had something to do with it."

As I described how he had shoved the pills up my nose and laughed as I suffered, I was bewildered by how someone I had married could be so evil. Even though we were separated, Darnell would always find me, and each encounter left me traumatized in some way. It was as though he couldn't stay away from me, but every time he came, he inflicted pain.

One day, Darnell and I were driving to a friend's house. As we approached our destination, he started arguing with me, his voice getting louder and more aggressive. I suspected it was because we were heading to a woman's house whom I believed he was cheating with, even though he denied it. As he continued to speed up, I panicked because he had forced me to use drugs before we left the house, and I was already hallucinating. He seemed to enjoy tormenting me when he knew I was vulnerable. As he drove faster, I screamed, pleading for him to let me out of the car. He responded by hitting me in the head repeatedly while calling me names and threatening me not to open the door. Terrified of what he might do once we arrived at the woman's house, I finally jumped out of the car.

A kind stranger let me into her home, where I waited for a Lyft to take me back to my apartment. When I got home, Darnell was already there, waiting for me with a look of anger and disbelief that I had dared to escape. He seemed to forget the punches, the threats, and the way he had tried to force me into submission.

I'll never forget Mother's Day, 2022. The night before, Darnell had abused me, hitting me and forcing me to use drugs, leaving me in unbearable pain. When my children came to visit the next morning, I was too high and injured to open the door. I could hear them knocking, but I couldn't move. Darnell, instead of helping, recorded a video of himself walking down the stairs, filming my children standing at the door as if it were some kind of sick joke. Later, he blamed me for not opening the door, mocking me for being too incapacitated to let my children in.

The pain of not being able to spend Mother's Day with my children because of Darnell's abuse still lingers. It was one of the worst feelings I've ever experienced, knowing that my abuser had involved my children in my suffering. He showed no remorse or empathy for the way he had taken that special day away from me, leaving me to relive the trauma every year since.

Every time Darnell abused me and left, I would cry out to God, screaming, "Why is he getting away with this?" My neighbors could hear me breaking down, and even though there was plenty of evidence of his abuse, law enforcement did nothing. Their negligence allowed the abuse to continue for years, leaving me with long-lasting mental and emotional scars. Loud noises still make me jump, and I have a deep fear of people getting too close, especially men. It took years for Darnell to finally go to jail, and even then, proving that I was the victim was an uphill battle.

I did everything I could to stay away from Darnell. I tried to move on with someone else, I begged for him to leave me alone, but he kept coming back, assaulting me and dragging me back into a cycle of trauma. He found a sick sense of power in terrorizing me, knowing that he could continue to abuse me and walk away without consequences.

I remember one day at my apartment when he had some food delivered after telling me he was homeless and had no money. I asked him who had sent the food because I didn't want just anyone knowing my address, and he exploded in rage. He hit me so hard in the head that I got a concussion. I drove myself to the hospital, where they confirmed the concussion and filed a police report. The authorities charged him, but he fled the state to avoid arrest.

Darnell had a habit of turning people against me, spreading lies, and making sure I was isolated. He'd mockingly tell me, "I always find a way to get away with everything," and when I cried and begged for help from law enforcement, it seemed like no one cared. The years of traumatic abuse left me in a constant state of fear, and Darnell seemed to take pleasure in seeing me broken. He'd record videos of me while I was under the influence of drugs he forced on me, enjoying my hallucinations and distress. The inhumane way he treated me was terrifying, and being around him felt like being near a wild, unpredictable monster.

I often found myself with no food, no money, and nowhere to go. Darnell would disappear for days, leaving me to starve. I had to beg strangers for food or sneak food at work, praying I wouldn't get caught. I couldn't understand how a person could treat another human being, especially someone they once vowed to love, with such cruelty.

There were times when I had business meetings or interviews, and Darnell would be in the same room, deliberately trying to distract me or instill fear. He didn't want me to share my story or succeed, but despite his threats and constant harassment, I refused to stay silent.

Darnell's appearances were always traumatic. He would force me to use drugs and then start arguments, knowing I was in a vulnerable state. Each time, I found myself fearing for my life as he continued to terrorize me with no regard for the damage he was causing.

I still struggle to comprehend how someone could be so merciless, so driven to destroy another person. But despite everything, I've held on to my faith. It's the only thing that has kept me grounded, reminding me to "Be still, and know that I am God."

Chapter 7: My Monster Has No Remorse

There was a time when I convinced myself that Darnell loved me, or at least he did at one point. I tried to rationalize his behavior, thinking maybe he just didn't know how to show it. But that illusion shattered every time he came home smelling of other women, only to crawl into bed with me. He'd insult me—say I stunk, that I wasn't attractive to him, that I needed to shower because I smelled bad. It was humiliating, cutting me deeper than the cruelest words. Then, within an hour, he'd be back, asking for sex, as if his previous words were never uttered. I soon realized that it wasn't about intimacy or connection; it was about control. He wasn't making love to me—he was using me to keep me bound to him, trapped in his cycle of narcissistic abuse. He feared the idea of me finding solace with another man, so he made sure to keep me tangled up in his grasp.

I could never understand how he could go out and cheat so blatantly, then come home and act as if nothing had happened. His twisted logic was baffling, even to me. It was so strange, so sickening, and yet there I was—helpless, feeling too trapped to escape. I went along with it because, at that time, he was still my husband. Even after our divorce, I found myself falling back into the same patterns. It wasn't love or desire; it was habit, survival, and an overwhelming sense of helplessness that kept me there. I was vulnerable, still searching for a way out, and it seemed easier to revert to what I knew rather than confront the reality of my situation.

Darnell's actions had nothing to do with love; they were rooted in disrespect. It was like he wanted to prove to himself that he could do whatever he wanted, and I would still be there, waiting for him. He knew exactly what he was doing. Every time I let him back in, I saw the satisfaction in his eyes—an affirmation that he still had control over me. I was nothing more than a pawn in his cruel game.

The worst were the nights he didn't come home. I would lay awake, my eyes wide open in the darkness, crying quietly so no one could hear. I cried because I couldn't comprehend how someone who claimed to love me could so effortlessly betray me. My tears were endless, a painful reminder of the broken promises and shattered dreams. The man I thought I loved was nothing more than a stranger who wore the face of someone I used to know.

Darnell's jealousy was another kind of torment. He could be out with other women, but the moment he suspected I might be talking to another man, he would erupt into fits of rage. His jealousy wasn't about love; it was about possession. He didn't want anyone else to have me because I was his—a toy he could discard and pick up whenever it suited him. He did everything in his power to keep me isolated. When friends would come around or people would ask me questions, he'd find ways to control the situation. He didn't like me being too open, sharing too much, because he knew the truth about what happened behind closed doors.

Even when I sought help from the police, it seemed like no one took me seriously. I showed them bruises, I gave them details, but they treated me like I was just some hysterical woman making things up. It didn't matter that I was telling the truth; Darnell had a way of charming his way out of trouble. He convinced them that I was just a crazy wife with an overactive imagination, and they let him walk away every time.

There was a period when we were homeless, living out of a van. I knew he was seeing another woman during that time, and I would often find myself being thrown out of the van and left at random grocery stores for hours. He'd come back when it suited him, always with some excuse, but I knew what he was doing. One time, during one of his fits of anger, he took my glasses and threw them out the window before driving off. I was left there, struggling to see, crying outside a grocery store. It was one of the countless times I felt completely powerless and abandoned.

As the abuse worsened, I saw sides of Darnell that terrified me. There were whispers, suspicious messages on his phone, and late-night trips to strange houses. The more I probed, the more I uncovered about his involvement in things far darker than infidelity. He and his best friend had connections to underage girls—girls they were giving drugs to, girls they were exploiting. One day, he took me to a house where a teenage girl climbed into the back seat of our car. Darnell handed her drugs without a second thought. The realization of what was happening hit me like a tidal wave, but when I confronted him, he brushed it off, telling me I didn't know what I was talking about. I tried reaching out to the authorities, even contacted the FBI, but nobody took me seriously. I was just a distressed woman with a far-fetched story, and Darnell continued to get away with it all.

The worst of it all was knowing that the man who shared my bed had no remorse. He was a monster hiding behind a human face, and there were times I thought he might kill me if I tried to leave or expose him. He had no problem hurting me to get what he wanted, and there was no limit to how far he would go to keep his dark secrets hidden.

It reached a breaking point when Darnell's best friend's house burned down. Rumors swirled that it was arson, and I asked him directly if he knew what had happened. His response chilled me to the bone. He looked me in the eyes and said, "I did it." I wanted to believe he was lying, but deep down, I knew he was telling the truth. He was capable of anything, and there was no line he wouldn't cross.

The day he confessed to getting his best friend's fiancée pregnant was the final betrayal. As we sat in a hotel room, Darnell spoke about it as though it were nothing more than a casual admission, no trace of shame or guilt. He had destroyed so many lives, mine included, without a second thought.

Darnell was a man who thrived on inflicting pain. Whether it was burning the inside of my throat with a pipe or using his fists to keep me in line, he found ways to remind me of my place. He wanted me broken, wanted me to believe I had nowhere else to go.

It's taken me years to finally see him for what he is—a monster with no remorse. For too long, I was trapped in the web he spun, afraid to speak out, afraid to leave. But now, I'm finding my voice, and I'm no longer afraid.

Chapter 8: Being Hunted & Divorcing My Monster

After divorcing Darnell, I felt a mix of relief and fear. The abuse was over, or so I thought. I soon started seeing someone new—a man I met at work. He was kind and attentive, offering a stark contrast to the nightmare I had just escaped. A few coworkers knew about my past with Darnell and that I was in the process of healing. On Valentine's Day, just two days before my divorce was finalized, this man expressed his feelings for me, making me feel hopeful for a fresh start. I felt optimistic about my future, but Darnell was not done with me.

A few weeks after the divorce, I began sharing my new relationship on social media. That was when Darnell reappeared. He started messaging me, professing his desire to reconcile, insisting we should have a baby and get remarried. His attempts at winning me back were relentless and disturbing. He kept repeating that no one else could have me and that he wasn't going to let me go. I was overwhelmed and still vulnerable from years of abuse. Despite my better judgment, I found myself drawn back into his orbit. I went to see him one night, and I vividly remember him saying, "We always end up back together. I've got a hold on you." That was when I recognized the grip of a trauma bond—a toxic attachment that kept me bound to him, despite the pain he caused.

For years, I had struggled to escape Darnell's reach. No matter how far I went or how many times I tried to leave, he always found a way back into my life. Every attempt to leave felt like fighting for my life, and each time I went back, it was because I was still chained to the trauma he inflicted on me. I was isolated, without a support system strong enough to help me break free. Even my own family could not understand the gravity of my situation, and some had even disowned me, believing I was choosing this life. Darnell used their disapproval to manipulate me, calling me a bad mother and telling me that my children would hate me. I felt trapped, ashamed, and alone.

Dating the new man was difficult because Darnell did everything in his power to sabotage the relationship. He found ways to scare him off and even had me call the man to end things while he listened. It was heartbreaking to hear the disappointment in the man's voice as I told him I didn't want to be with him anymore. Darnell was elated at my heartbreak. He thrived on my misery and would go to any lengths to keep me from finding happiness. I was continually pulled back into his darkness.

One night, after we were divorced, I went to see Darnell at a hotel where he was staying. He was high on drugs, and when I questioned his behavior, he became violent. He pushed me into the room, his fists striking my chest, forcing me back. He yelled at me to get out, his rage filling the room. It was then I understood: the divorce hadn't changed him. He was still the same monstrous person I had known for years. In that moment, I felt the weight of all the confusion, stress, and pain I had endured crash down on me.

The day before I filed for divorce, Darnell called me, saying he knew I was going to do something "stupid" like ending our marriage. His abuse continued even as we were living in different states. He had affairs, abandoned me repeatedly, and his treatment of me had only grown more disrespectful. One time, during our divorce proceedings, he showed up in another woman's car. It was an open display of disrespect, but it motivated me to push forward with the divorce.

After the divorce, when I attempted to rebuild my life, Darnell remained a looming presence. There was one incident where I found out that he was still connected to a woman through a phone plan. When I confronted him about it and attempted to reach out to her to clarify that Darnell and I were back together, he flew into a rage. He warned me that if I made the call, he would kill me. When I tried to reach for the phone, he attacked me. He wrapped his hands around my neck and threw me to the floor. He repeatedly choked me, yanked my hair, and slammed me into the bed. The strength of his rage was terrifying, and I was powerless against him.

In those moments, I realized I was living with a monster—a man who took pleasure in hurting me. The physical and emotional abuse continued, leaving me in constant fear. I began to think the only way to escape was to end his life because the abuse was becoming more unbearable. Each blow, every time he threw me to the ground, I cried out to God, asking why Darnell was allowed to torment me without consequence. I reached out for help, filed reports, but nothing changed. The system failed to protect me, and I felt completely abandoned.

Darnell's cruelty was relentless, but I had to find a way to break the chains and reclaim my life. Each step was a battle, but it was one I was determined to win. I had to muster all my strength to sever the trauma bond and set myself free from the cycle of abuse. Though I was fearful, I slowly began to rebuild, piece by piece, and promised myself that I would never again let the monster back into my life. The journey to freedom was long and painful, but I knew I deserved peace, love, and a life free from fear. I had to reclaim my power and learn to live again, one step at a time.

Chapter 9: Breaking Free from the Monster

As I sit down to write this chapter, I find myself reflecting on the journey that has brought me to this moment—a moment of safety, healing, and empowerment. It's been a long road, filled with pain and struggle, but I've learned that it's okay to be alone. I had to come to terms with this truth, especially after falling into the depths of bonding with my abuser.

To anyone who finds themselves in a situation like I once was, I want to say this: You are capable of breaking free. You can thrive and survive. Remember how amazing you were before the abuse entered your life. Recall your intelligence, your strength, and your brilliance. Find the courage within yourself to seek a good support system, both mentally and physically. Leave for good and maintain no contact with Darnell. I have moved on with my life, learned to love myself again, and discovered what it means to truly be happy and safe.

Being alive to write this book is a testimony in itself. There were countless times when I believed Darnell would succeed in taking my life, as he was relentless in his attempts to strip away my existence. But here I am, transformed by the passion and energy I've poured into telling my story—a story of survival.

As I heal from the traumatic abuse I endured, I have finally begun to process what happened to me. It's not an easy journey, but it is necessary. I strive to make an impact in others' lives, to show them how to escape the darkness, how to stay out, and that there is a greater life waiting for them after abuse.

What I have learned, and the best advice I can offer to other trauma survivors, is this: Celebrate your good days, and on your bad days, give yourself grace. You were a victim, and you suffered trauma—mental, physical, verbal, and emotional. Healing takes time. I hope that as you read my book, you find empowerment and the strength to speak out about your experiences. Know that you deserve better, and you can overcome anything.

Reflecting on the days spent crying, I remember the pain of reliving the trauma inflicted by my abuser. Darnell's actions were a relentless storm, and I often hoped I would never encounter him again. I wish for him to serve his time in jail and to never find me again. No one should endure the torture and torment I faced at the hands of my monster.

Forgiveness is a complicated journey, one that will take time. I have the right to heal from the physical, emotional, and verbal attacks he inflicted on me. As time passes, I know I will find peace. I have finally mustered the courage, after years of fighting for my life, to break free mentally and physically.

I think back to the days spent in the shelter, writing this book while battling the memories of my past. I recall the bathroom breaks at work, where I would cry uncontrollably, the pain bubbling to the surface as I wrote excerpts of my story. Each tear represented a memory, a moment of anguish that shaped my experience.

Revisiting the places where Darnell terrorized me took immense strength. I remember standing outside the last hotel room where he abused me, feeling the weight of every vicious attack wash over me again. In those moments, I was reminded of the isolation he forced upon me, how I felt helpless, and yet, it was during that reign of terror that I found my strength and began to plan my escape.

Many nights, I cried out to God, asking why this was happening to me. But I also remember God keeping me safe, granting me the strength to heal and keep pushing forward until I was finally free from my monster.

I have come to understand that what Darnell did to me was not my fault. I often blamed myself, thinking that if I had done things differently, I could have avoided his abuse. But I've realized that Darnell's issues were his own, and they had nothing to do with the wonderful person I am.

To all the victims and survivors out there, please remember this: Never blame yourself for what your monster did to you. I know I am just one of many women who have laid down with a monster and lived to tell the story. You can escape and go on to live a great life. Your life is not over; God has something better in store for you.

I never imagined I could encounter such danger as I did when I entered into a relationship with Darnell. The trauma, the pain—it lingers, but over time, it will fade. The horror I experienced will forever be etched in my memory, but I refuse to let it define me.

There are many monsters out there, masked as good people, whose only goal is to disrupt your peace, make you unhappy, and inflict pain. But remember, you are the prize, not the trash they may try to make you feel like. If you're facing your monster, I encourage you to find the strength to defeat it.

For years, I lived in a cycle of leaving and returning to Darnell, paralyzed by fear of the unknown. But eventually, God provided me the strength I needed to fully disconnect from him. Now, I live fearlessly, happily, and productively.

If I can do it, so can you. Together, we can break the cycle and find a path toward an abundantly blessed life.

Dear Reader,

As you embark on this journey through my story in *Sleeping with a Monster: My Story of Survival,* I want to take a moment to speak directly to you. Writing this book has been a deeply personal experience, one filled with reflection, pain, and ultimately, healing. It's a journey that I hope resonates with you and brings you comfort, strength, and inspiration.

I want you to know that you are not alone. The feelings of isolation, fear, and despair that accompany the experience of abuse can be overwhelming. I've walked that painful path and have felt the weight of darkness pressing down on me. Yet, amidst that darkness, I discovered a flicker of hope.

In sharing my story, my greatest desire is for you to recognize the incredible strength within yourself. There were times when I doubted my worth, when I believed the lies that my abuser fed me. But as I began to reclaim my life, I learned that my past did not define my future. Each day was a step toward healing, a step away from the monster who sought to steal my joy.

You are capable of more than you realize. You possess the power to break free from the chains of your past, just as I did. It takes courage, and it may not happen overnight, but you have the strength to thrive. Remember the person you were before the trauma, the amazing individual who deserves to be loved, respected, and cherished.

I encourage you to surround yourself with a supportive community. Seek out those who uplift you, who empower you to heal and grow. It is vital to find your voice and speak your truth, for there is immense power in sharing your story. Know that it's okay to grieve, to feel the pain, and to give yourself grace on your healing journey.

As you read my story, I hope you feel empowered to confront your own monsters, to find the strength to walk away, and to embrace a future filled with possibilities. You are worthy of love, happiness, and a life free from fear.

Thank you for allowing me to share my journey with you. I am honored to stand alongside you as we navigate the path to healing together. You are stronger than you know, and I believe in your ability to create a life filled with hope and joy.

With love and encouragement,

Aneta Sproles

Survival Guide for Domestic Violence Survivors

This guide offers practical advice and tools to help survivors of domestic violence rebuild their lives with confidence and safety. Each section provides actionable steps to help recognize harmful patterns, develop a safety plan, work towards independence, and cultivate self-care habits for healing.

1. Recognizing Red Flags in Relationships

Identifying abusive behaviors can be difficult, especially when emotions are involved. Here are common red flags to be aware of:

- Control and Isolation: Your partner tries to control your actions, choices, or limits your contact with friends and family.
- Unpredictable Temper: Displays sudden anger or violence, often followed by apologies or promises to change.
- Verbal and Emotional Abuse: Uses hurtful language, belittling, or manipulative tactics to make you feel small or worthless.
- Excessive Jealousy and Possessiveness: Your partner constantly accuses you of cheating or being unfaithful without cause.
- Blame Shifting: Refuses to take responsibility for hurtful actions, instead blaming you or others.

Tip: Trust your intuition. If something doesn't feel right or if you're uncomfortable in your relationship, don't dismiss these feelings.

2. Developing a Safety Plan

Having a plan is crucial, especially if you're considering leaving an abusive relationship. Here are steps to develop a solid safety plan:

- Identify a Safe Place: Determine a safe location to go

to in case of immediate danger, such as a trusted friend
or family member's home, or a local shelter.

- Pack an Emergency Bag: Prepare a bag with essentials
  like clothes, medications, identification, important
  documents, cash, and a phone charger. Store it
  somewhere accessible.

- Create a Code Word: Arrange a code word with
  trusted friends or family members so you can discreetly
  signal for help if you're in danger.

- Document Abuse: Keep a record of abusive incidents,
  including photos, screenshots of messages, or medical
  reports, to use as evidence if needed.

- Memorize Hotlines: Save emergency contacts like the
  National Domestic Violence Hotline
  (1-800-799-7233) on a hidden or alternative phone if
  possible.

Tip: Make copies of any critical documents you might need,
such as birth certificates, driver's licenses, and social security
cards, and leave them with someone you trust.

3. Steps to Regain Independence

Leaving an abusive relationship is just the first step.
Rebuilding your life and independence takes time and patience.
Here are steps to help you regain control:

- Financial Independence: Open a personal bank
  account if possible. Look into programs that offer
  financial assistance, job training, and support for
  survivors.

- Secure Housing: If you need a place to stay, contact

local shelters or housing assistance programs that offer temporary or transitional housing.

- Establish New Boundaries: Practice saying "no" and create boundaries with others, especially those who may remind you of your past or bring negativity into your life.
- Pursue Education or Training: Enrolling in courses, vocational programs, or training can help you build new skills and boost self-confidence, setting the foundation for a stable future.

Tip: Take small steps each day toward your goals. Building independence may seem daunting, but gradual progress leads to lasting change.

4. Self-Care Routines for Healing

Self-care is essential for recovery and mental well-being. Establishing routines can support you through the healing process and bring peace to your everyday life.

- Daily Affirmations: Start each day with positive affirmations like "I am worthy of love and respect" or "I am stronger than my circumstances."
- Physical Care: Engage in regular activities that keep you active, like walking, stretching, or light exercise, to relieve stress and boost mood.
- Emotional Processing: Journaling, art, or speaking with a therapist can help you process emotions and work through trauma. Expressing your feelings is a form of self-care.
- Social Connections: Seek out supportive friends,

family, or support groups. Having a circle of understanding people can make a significant difference in your journey.

- Set Boundaries with Technology: If contact with your abuser continues via social media or phone, consider blocking or changing accounts to protect your mental space.

Tip: Healing is not linear. Allow yourself to take breaks and don't be too hard on yourself. Small, consistent acts of self-care are powerful in building resilience.

Conclusion

The path to recovery is a journey of courage and self-compassion. Taking even small steps to recognize abuse, plan for safety, regain independence, and focus on self-care can lead to a life of renewed strength, freedom, and healing.

Empowering Women To
Thrive, Heal, & Be Free
AUTHOR & SPEAKER
ANETA SPROLES

ADE RECOVERY & TRANSITIONAL LIVING
DFW Domestic Violence Program
community.
Domestic
Violence
Resources
ADE Recovery &
Transitional Living
Protective Order Assistance
Immediate & Long Term Shelter
Resources
Counseling
Job Placement Assistance
Further Education Resources
Food
Resources for Children
For More Info:
Contact Program Director
Aneta Sproles
737-304-2120
Email:
ADERecoveryOutreachTL@gmail.com

Resource Guide for Domestic Violence Survivors

This resource guide is designed to provide support for survivors of domestic violence. It includes various resources organized by type, offering emotional, financial, and legal support to aid in the journey to recovery and independence.

1. Emotional Support

- National Domestic Violence Hotline
  - Phone: 1-800-799-7233 (SAFE)

- - Website: www.thehotline.org[1]
  - Description: 24/7 confidential support for survivors, including counseling and resources for crisis situations. Text and chat options available.
- RAINN (Rape, Abuse & Incest National Network)
  - Phone: 1-800-656-4673 (HOPE)
  - Website: www.rainn.org[2]
  - Description: Free, confidential counseling for survivors of sexual violence and domestic abuse. Provides access to trained professionals and resources.
- Therapy and Support Groups
  - Website: Psychology Today (www.psychologytoday.com[3]) for locating therapists and support groups
  - Description: Use this directory to find licensed therapists who specialize in trauma and abuse recovery, as well as support groups for survivors.

2. Financial Assistance

- National Coalition Against Domestic Violence (NCADV)
  - Website: www.ncadv.org[4]
  - Description: Offers resources and referrals to

---

1. http://www.thehotline.org

2. http://www.rainn.org

3. http://www.psychologytoday.com

4. http://www.ncadv.org

local organizations that provide emergency shelter, relocation assistance, and help with essential needs for survivors.

- Women's Independence Scholarship Program (WISP)
  - Website: www.wispinc.org[5]
  - Description: Provides financial support for survivors of domestic violence seeking education and job training, helping them work toward financial independence.
- Temporary Assistance for Needy Families (TANF)
  - Website: www.benefits.gov[6]
  - Description: State-administered financial assistance for low-income families, including survivors of domestic violence. Assistance includes funds for housing, food, and job training.
- Local Food Banks and Shelters
  - Website: Feeding America (www.feedingamerica.org[7])
  - Description: Find local food banks and shelters through Feeding America's directory for temporary assistance with food, clothing, and shelter needs.

3. Legal Help

- National Network to End Domestic Violence (NNEDV)

---

5. http://www.wispinc.org

6. http://www.benefits.gov

7. http://www.feedingamerica.org

- Website: www.nnedv.org[8]
- Description: Provides links to free and low-cost legal services, as well as advocacy programs. NNEDV also offers guidance on how to obtain restraining orders, custody issues, and other legal protections.

- Legal Aid Society
  - Website: www.lsc.gov[9]
  - Description: A nonprofit organization that provides legal services to survivors of domestic violence. Includes services for family law, housing rights, and protective orders.

- American Bar Association (ABA) Commission on Domestic and Sexual Violence
  - Website: www.americanbar.org[10]
  - Description: ABA's network of pro-bono and low-cost attorneys who specialize in assisting survivors with legal representation for divorce, child custody, and protective orders.

- State and Local Government Websites
  - Website: USA.gov
  - Description: Access your state or county website for information on local protective services, housing programs, and emergency assistance programs specifically for survivors.

4. Additional Resources

---

8. http://www.nnedv.org

9. http://www.lsc.gov

10. http://www.americanbar.org

- National Child Abuse Hotline
  - Phone: 1-800-422-4453
  - Website: www.childhelp.org[11]
  - Description: Offers crisis intervention, information, and referrals to thousands of emergencies, social service, and support resources. Assistance is available for children affected by abuse.
- Love is Respect
  - Phone: 1-866-331-9474
  - Text: Text LOVEIS to 22522
  - Website: www.loveisrespect.org[12]
  - Description: Specializes in resources and support for young people and teens in abusive relationships, including counseling and educational resources.
- National Alliance on Mental Illness (NAMI)
  - Phone: 1-800-950-6264
  - Website: www.nami.org[13]
  - Description: Provides mental health resources and support groups for those affected by trauma, helping survivors manage mental health needs that may arise from abuse.

Note to Readers

---

11. http://www.childhelp.org

12. http://www.loveisrespect.org

13. http://www.nami.org

These resources are available to provide immediate and long-term support for survivors of domestic violence. If you or someone you know is in immediate danger, please call 911.

About the Author

Aneta Sproles is a passionate advocate for survivors of domestic abuse and the founder of ADE Recovery & Transitional Living, a non-profit organization dedicated to helping individuals rebuild their lives after trauma. Drawing from her personal experiences of enduring and overcoming abuse, Aneta channels her strength and resilience into her writing and advocacy work. *Sleeping with a Monster: My Story of Survival* is her powerful memoir that sheds light on the realities of domestic violence, offering hope and inspiration to those facing similar challenges. Through her journey, Aneta encourages others to break the silence, seek help, and find their own path to healing.